Sticker Puzzle CHRISTMAS

Susannah Leigh
Illustrated by Brenda Haw

Contents

Edited by Jenny Tyler and Catriona Clarke
Design coordinator: Laura Parker
Additional design: Vicky Arrowsmith

About this book

This book is about a girl named Kira and her Christmas adventure. There are puzzles to solve and stickers to add on every double page. You'll find the stickers and the answers at the back of the book.

Kira loves everything about Christmas — but she lives in a very warm place. She has never seen snow. So this year she has written a letter to Santa.

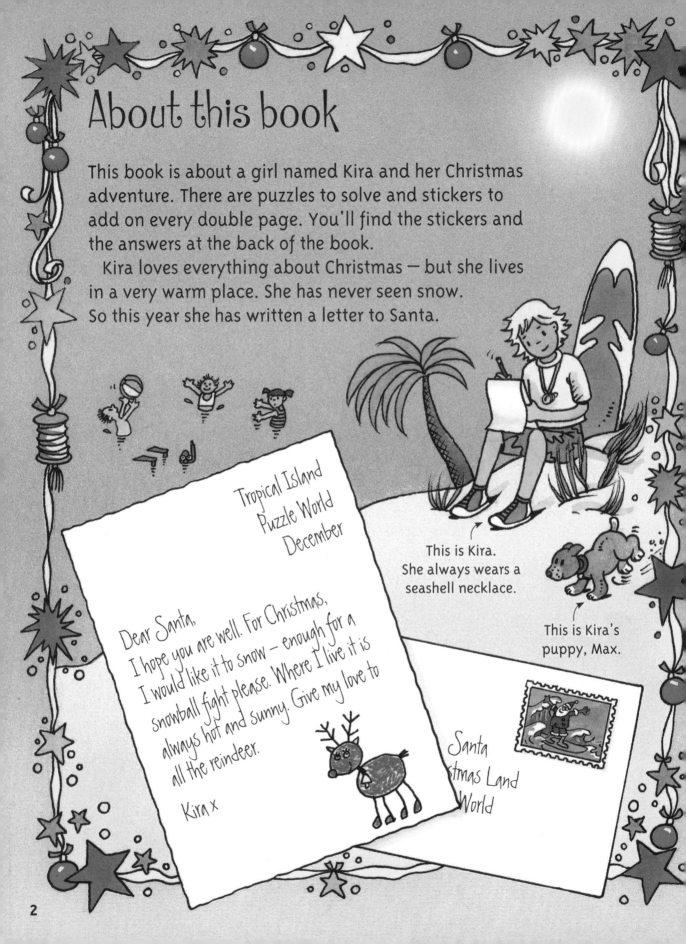

Tropical Island
Puzzle World
December

Dear Santa,
I hope you are well. For Christmas,
I would like it to snow — enough for a
snowball fight please. Where I live it is
always hot and sunny. Give my love to
all the reindeer.

Kira x

Santa
...stmas Land
...World

This is Kira.
She always wears a
seashell necklace.

This is Kira's
puppy, Max.

Things to spot

Can you spot one of these Christmas decorations on each double page?

Chocolate bell

Toy Santa

Crib

Christmas cracker

Stocking

Reindeer

Lantern

Mistletoe

Star

Candy cane

Ornament

Garland

Gingerbread house

Christmas presents

There is a little wrapped Christmas present to spot on every double page.

Gingerbread men

There is also one jolly gingerbread man to find on every double page.

Surf's up!

One morning, just before Christmas, Kira was out surfing. Riding a giant wave, she had a great view of the beach, and all her friends. There was Emma, building a sandcastle, and Ben, licking an ice cream. Maria and Carlos were doing handstands. Her puppy, Max, was digging in the sand. Then, Kira saw something that looked very out of place.

Can you spot Kira's friends? Stick an arrow by each one. What else has Kira seen? Stick a snowflake next to it.

Rio's story

...now I have lost my magic bell. Without it, I can't fly back home to Christmas Land, and Santa promised —

Kira could hardly believe her eyes. She rode a wave back to the beach and raced through the palm trees. Sure enough, there stood a little reindeer, looking lost and frightened.

"What are you doing here?" Kira asked kindly. "Can I help you?"

She hadn't really expected the reindeer to answer, but when he did, Kira found she wasn't surprised. She knew magical things could happen at Christmas time. But the reindeer's story was all mixed up and Kira had trouble making sense of it.

Can you understand the reindeer's story? Use the number stickers to put it all in the right order.

...from a boy named Lucas, who has never seen the sea.

Hitching a lift

When Kira heard Rio's story, she was worried. "Christmas Eve
is tomorrow," she said. "We have to get you back to Christmas
Land so you can pull Santa's sleigh."

Rio shook his head sadly. "I can't find my bell anywhere."

"It will be OK, Rio. I'll help you look for it," said Kira.

They walked along the beach searching for the bell, but they
couldn't find it.

"We'll have to find some other way to get you home," said Kira. They had come to the port, busy with boats of all kinds. Suddenly, Kira had an idea.

"These boats go all over the world," she said. "One might be heading your way, Rio!"

Is there a boat that Rio could hitch a lift with? Stick a white arrow next to the most likely one.

Chilly voyage

Kira helped Rio aboard, but the boat set sail before she could jump off again.

"Oh no! Rio, what am I going to do?" she gasped.

"Don't worry," Rio said. "When you get back, it will seem as if you've been away no time at all. Santa's Christmas magic will see to that. Now, we'd better hide in these barrels so nobody finds us."

After a choppy voyage at sea, the barrels were loaded onto a plane...

... and then a train. They rattled through the night, and came to the edge of an icy world.

Brr. I'm cold!

Take my blanket.

Christmas Land! Hop on my back, Kira, and I'll carry you across the ice.

CHRISTMAS LAND

Can you find a way to Christmas Land? Stick snowshoes along the route - and avoid the cracks!

Light show

Rio and Kira scrambled ashore. In the distance they saw swirly lights, dancing across the morning sky.

Rio kicked his hooves in delight. "Those are the magic lights of Christmas Land, and it's not far from here to Santa's house. We're nearly there!"

They wandered among tall pillars of ice in the frosty glow. Then, Kira saw one of the pillars move. Looking closer, she realized that they were surrounded by lots of polar bears!

How many polar bears can you spot? Stick a frosty icicle by each one.

Polar slide

The polar bears came closer and closer. Kira was afraid, until one of them shouted, "Hello, Rio!" The bears were eager to hear Rio's story. "Lost your magic bell, eh?" said the biggest bear. "That's bad news. Don't worry, Rio. We'll take you to Snowman Village — it's not far from there to Santa's. Hop on our backs and hang on tight. It's going to be a slippery ride, avoiding all the fallen trees and snoozing seals."

Can you find a way down the icy maze to the village below? Stick on sliding bears to show the way.

SNOWMAN VILLAGE

Snow ho ho

With a whiz and a whoosh, they slipped to the end of the slide. "That was fun!" cried Kira.

"We'd better leave you here," whispered the bears. "The snow people get nervous around us."

Kira stared around in amazement. There were snow men and snow women, snow babies and snow pets. And what's more, there were piles and piles of snow!

"Just what I wanted," she cried. "Enough snow for a big —"

"Snowball fight!" Rio finished. He introduced Kira to the snow people, and everyone got ready to play.

Who is on Kira's team and who is on Rio's? Stick the right team badge by each player.

Let's play!

Find your teams... and plenty of snowballs!

17

Forest trail

After the fight, Kira collapsed, breathless. "Who won?" she laughed.

   "I have no idea!" Rio giggled. "But wasn't it fun?"

   "Great fun! Oh, but Rio, it's getting late and starting to snow. Let's get you back to Santa."

   "OK," Rio said. "Come on. Santa lives on the other side of Frosty Forest."

They walked through frosty pines and snowy glades...

...until they found a snug little house.

Rio and Kira looked inside.

Rio gasped at what he heard. "Do you know who that is, Kira? And do you remember what he asked for? I completely forgot!"

"I remember," Kira said. "And I think I have something he wants."

Who is the boy? Stick a pink arrow next to something that Kira could give him.

Tree trouble

"Lucas can have my seashell."

Rio took the seashell. "Thank you, Kira. Santa can take it with him tonight."

The two friends went on through the forest. Soon, they came upon a beautiful sight: a small clearing that sparkled with decorated Christmas trees. But the littlest tree was dull and bare, and beside it stood a worried old elf.

"Oh dear. I've lost the decorations for this little tree."

"We can help," Kira said kindly. "What have you lost?"

"It's quite a list: five red apples, two blue ornaments, a gold star, one white ornament, four popcorn strings, three green ornaments and an angel doll."

Stick a red arrow by all the missing things. Then, decorate the top of the little tree with a gold star.

Toy maze

As Kira placed the star on top of the little tree, it suddenly lit up with magic lights.

"Thank you!" the old elf called, as Kira and Rio waved goodbye.

At the edge of the forest there was a little red train waiting for them.

"We're nearly there," Rio cried. "We just need to hop on this train. Do you think you can drive it to that red door over there, Kira?"

"I think so, but we'd better watch out for those giant toys."

Help Kira and Rio find the best route by sticking snowflakes along the track.

Meet the family

They hopped off the train, and Rio turned to Kira. "I'll take you to meet my family before we go to see Santa. I hope he's not upset with me."

Rio and Kira stepped into a warm stable.

"Rio! Where have you been?" called a reindeer.

"Hi Dad, I went to Tropical Island but I lost my magic bell," Rio said.

Rudy

Rex

Rose

Rolf

"Oh, Rio. We were so worried about you!"

"I'm sorry," Rio said. "This is Kira. She helped me get home."

"And I think I can guess your names," said Kira, smiling.

Can you tell which reindeer is which?
Stick the correct label next to each one.

Wonderful workshop

The reindeer laughed. "Clever, Kira! Do you want to meet Santa?" Kira nodded, and Rio led her to Santa's workshop. Elves were busy making toys and singing Christmas songs.

Then…

"Ho ho ho!" boomed a jolly voice.
"Santa, it's really you!" Kira cried.
But Rio wasn't so sure about seeing Santa.
"I'm sorry I flew off without telling you," he whispered. "And I lost my magic bell."

CYCLE BELL

TREE BELL

JINGLE BELL

FAIRY BELL

CHRISTMAS BELL

REINDEER BELL
(MAGIC)

"I know you were only trying to help, Rio," said Santa kindly. "Now, let's find you another magic bell for tonight."

"You mean...?" Rio began.

"Yes," Santa said. "You're just in time to lead my sleigh. Kira can come too. Now, there are lots of bells here, but only one is magic."

Stick an orange arrow by Rio's magic bell.
Then, add some more bells to Santa's workshops.

Christmas Eve!

Later, on the most magical night of the year, Rio proudly pulled Santa's sleigh through the starry sky.

Kira looked down with delight from her seat next to Santa. "I can see the whole world from up here!" she cried. "Look, there are the snow people — and the polar bears, the little old elf and his Christmas trees, the train track, and Lucas's house. Don't forget to give him his shell, Santa!"

Put a sticker next to everything that Kira has spotted. Be sure to use the right sticker for each part of Christmas Land!

Magical morning

When Santa finally dropped Kira back home, no time at all had passed and everyone was still on the beach. Kira began to wonder if she had imagined her magical adventure.

But on Christmas morning, she found a special present in her room. She hadn't imagined it after all. Her puppy, Max, had a surprise for her, too.

Who is the special present from?

What has Max found?

Look back through the book and stick a Christmas star where he found it.

Answers

Pages 4-5

Kira's friends are circled here. Kira has also spotted a reindeer hiding in the trees.

Pages 6-7

1. Hello my name is Rio, I'm Santa's littlest reindeer.
2. This year Santa got a letter…
3. …from a boy named Lucas, who has never seen the sea.
4. Now, Lucas wanted a seashell for Christmas. Santa wondered if he'd have time to find one, so I thought I would surprise Santa by…
5. …flying over here and getting one. But…
6. …now I have lost my magic bell. Without it, I can't fly back home to Christmas Land, and Santa promised —
7. — that I could pull the sleigh on Christmas Eve. Oh dear!

Pages 8-9

This boat has just delivered trees from Christmas Land, and is about to sail back there.

Pages 10-11

Pages 12-13

There are 12 bears hiding in the ice.

Pages 14-15

Pages 16-17

Kira's team wears red and yellow badges. Rio's team wears blue and yellow badges.

Pages 18-19

The boy in the house is Lucas, who wrote to Santa asking for a seashell. Rio can take Kira's shell to give to Lucas.

Pages 20-21

The missing decorations are circled here.

Pages 22-23

The train must follow the tracks this way to get to the other side.

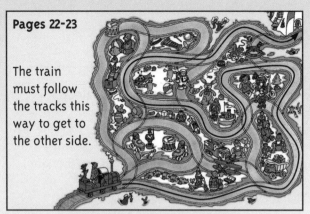

Pages 24-25

Rolf is the reindeer with the blue nose.
Rose has a ring in her nose.
Rex has a glossy black tail.
Rudy has a red nose.
Rita is the reindeer with a bow on her tail.
Roger has a silvery tail.

Pages 26-27

Rio's magic reindeer bell is on the table with the food.

Pages 28-29

All the people and parts of Christmas Land that Kira has spotted are circled here.

Did you spot everything?

Did you find a gingerbread man on every double page?

And did you find the Christmas presents?

Page 30

The special present is a snowball from her friend Rio.
Max has found Rio's lost reindeer bell. He found it near the beach on page 6.

This list shows where the Christmas decorations are hidden.

Pages	Objects
4	Ornament
7	Mistletoe
9	Lantern
11	Candy cane
12	Christmas cracker
14	Gingerbread house
16	Star
19	Toy Santa
20	Crib
23	Stocking
25	Reindeer
26	Chocolate bell
29	Garland

This edition first published in 2014, by Usborne Publishing Ltd, Usborne House, 83-85 Saffron Hill, London, EC1N 8RT, England. www.usborne.com Copyright © 2014, 2008 Usborne Publishing Ltd. The name Usborne and the devices 🔅⊕ are Trade Marks of Usborne Publishing Ltd.

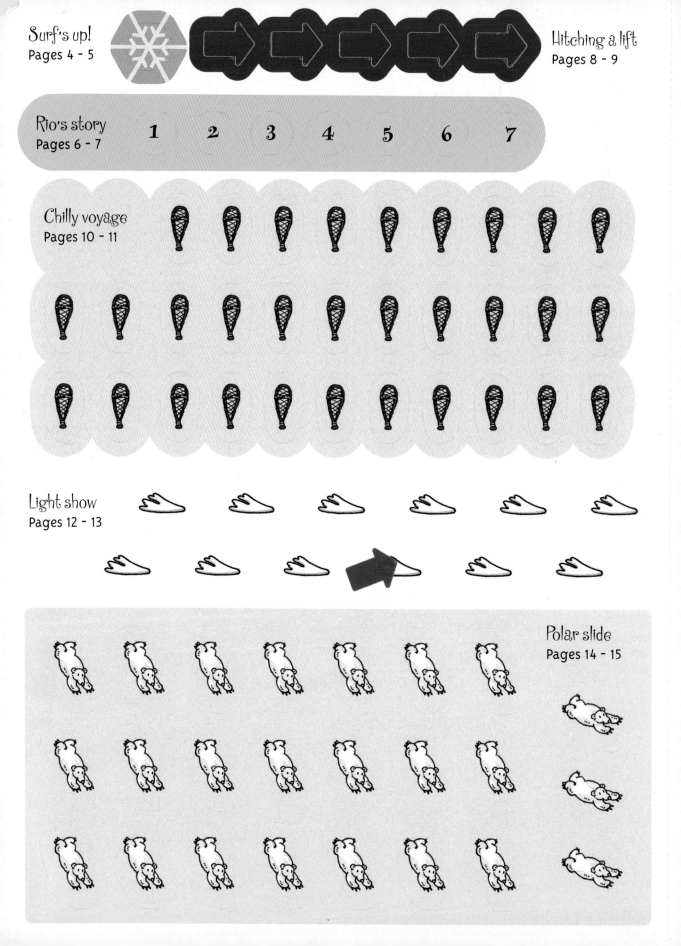

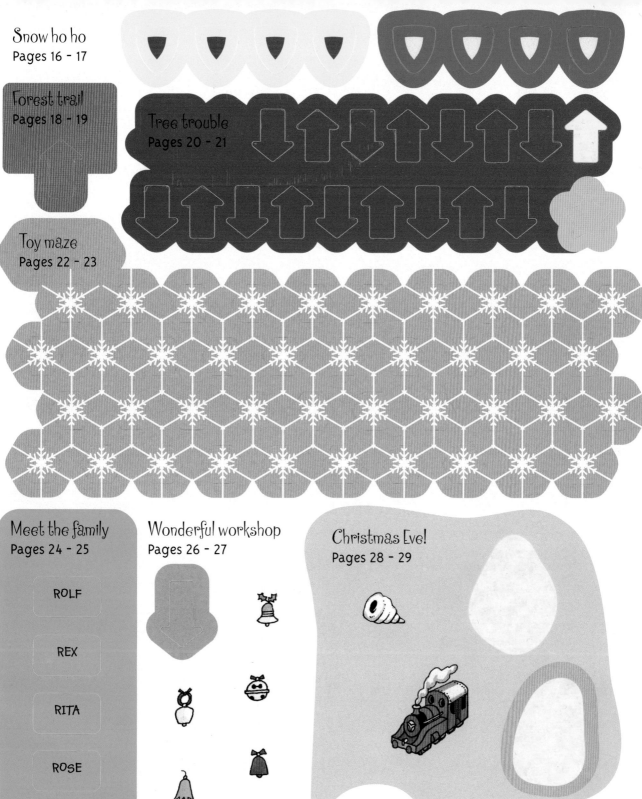

Snow ho ho
Pages 16 – 17

Forest trail
Pages 18 – 19

Tree trouble
Pages 20 – 21

Toy maze
Pages 22 – 23

Meet the family
Pages 24 – 25

ROLF

REX

RITA

ROSE

RUDY

ROGER

Wonderful workshop
Pages 26 – 27

Christmas Eve!
Pages 28 – 29

Magical
morning
Page 30